Can the Market Speak?

Can the Market Speak?

Campbell Jones

Winchester, UK
Washington, USA

First published by Zero Books, 2013
Zero Books is an imprint of John Hunt Publishing Ltd., Laurel House, Station Approach,
Alresford, Hants, SO24 9JH, UK
office1@jhpbooks.net
www.johnhuntpublishing.com
www.zero-books.net

For distributor details and how to order please visit the 'Ordering' section on our website.

Design: Stuart Davies

Printed and bound by CPI Group (UK) Ltd, Croydon, CR0 4YY

We operate a distinctive and ethical publishing philosophy in all
areas of our business, from our global network of authors to
production and worldwide distribution.

CONTENTS

Acknowledgements

I would like thank my colleagues at the Centre for Philosophy and Political Economy at the University of Leicester for providing such a vibrant and generous intellectual environment for so many years. Thanks also to students on my Fantasies of Finance course at the University of Auckland for feedback on the first complete presentation of this book and for so much valuable engagement and encouragement. More generally, thanks to my new colleagues and students who are the University of Auckland. You have renewed my hope in the future of the university.

Various aspects of this book have been presented at conferences and other public occasions over the past four years and I am grateful for all of the feedback received. Particular thanks to Mikkel Thorup and his colleagues in the Department of the History of Ideas at Aarhus University for the kind invitation to present my work in Denmark in early 2012.

Jai Bentley-Payne, Christian Olaf Christiansen, Shanti Daellenbach, Anna-Maria Murtola and André Spicer read a complete draft of this book and offered many valuable suggestions. I remain responsible for the many failings that remain.

For her constant support, for insisting that I finish this book, and for so many other gifts, I thank Anna-Maria.

I

The spirit is a bone

If 'the market' is an ever present reality in daily life today, it is a mysterious and enigmatic presence. Being at once omnipresent yet ineffable, it is not surprising that attempts to symbolise the market have been so fantastic. This book investigates the idea that the market might be able to speak, and along with this that the market is a kind of person, above all the kind of person that should be listened to and obeyed.

When a body is attributed speech, it is given much more than voice. The power of speech tends to bring with it an idea of personhood, in such a way that a body that speaks is taken to have a soul or 'spirit' from which that speech issues. The attribution of speech typically involves the attribution of personhood and an interiority which issues forth a motivating force or will. Thus when it is said that something like the market can speak, it is also generally attributed particular subjective states. With the attribution of speech comes the idea that the market can want, will, desire, and respond to the actions of us mere mortals. Giving speech to the market comes hand in hand with giving the market a sense of personhood. What follows is therefore an investigation of the attribution to the market of the capacity of speech and at the same time the treatment of the market as a kind of person.

The figure by which speech is attributed to imaginary or absent persons or to bodies or abstractions not normally considered to be able to speak is known as prosopopoeia. This takes place when human or non-human animals are attributed the power of speech, and also when material objects or abstract entities are treated as if they can speak. Prosopopoeia of the market happens when, for example, it is said that the market has spoken, has given its verdict, or when it is said that one needs to listen to the market. Alongside this prosopopoeia comes a personification. Personification of the market happens when, for example, it is said that the market 'wants', 'demands' or 'needs' this or that, and also when market analysts interpret the market as bearer of intentions behind its surface manifestations, signs that originate from the deep interior will of the market.

In 1936 John Maynard Keynes spoke of the way that participants in markets are driven by a spontaneous optimism that goes well beyond mathematical expectations of reward. Drawing on ancient ideas, he called this set of motivations the 'animal spirits'. In recent years there has been considerable interest in such ideas, in order to understand market volatility and also to provide a more realistic picture of market actors. Thus there have been various efforts to 'put people back in' to accounts of how markets work. In the areas of behavioural economics and behavioural finance there have been various efforts in recent years to understand market behaviour based on a more realistic conception of the human subject, in which participants in markets are taken as persons with all of their properly human frailties and limitations.[1]

The goal of this book is not to put people back into markets, but almost exactly the opposite. Today the market has taken on a life of its own, and has become too much like a person. Hence the focus is not on putting people into markets, but rather on understanding the idea of the market as a kind of person. Today the market itself has become an agent in its own right and has been invested with animal spirits.

The prosopopoeia of the market raises profound philosophical questions regarding who and what can speak. According to a way of thinking that goes back at least as far as Aristotle, it is thought that humans alone possess the power of speech. It is because of the presence of this idea that Spinoza, for example, will say that 'those who do not know the true causes of things confuse everything and without any conflict of mind feign that both trees and men speak'.[2] To imagine speech where there is none, to think that things other than humans could speak, is to take a whimsical flight of fancy, if not to display signs of delusion or outright madness. In the prosopopoeia of the market rests if not a madness then a peculiar cultural poetics that becomes visible in the way that entities such as the market are widely symbolised.

The personification of the market also raises complex questions regarding what it means for specific bodies to be counted as persons. The question of what it means to be a person is one of the founding questions of philosophy, and questions of the creation or the invention of persons have been central in philosophy and social theory over the past century. Recent considerations around 'the question of the subject' have raised powerful challenges to common ways of thinking about what it means to imagine things such as persons, and provides important grounds for the investigation to follow. I will seek to show that questions of personhood and the subject find fertile grounds not only in the consideration of bodies that most obviously appear to be persons – you, me, specific others. Questions of personhood and the subject can equally illuminate the dynamics of the attribution of personhood to entities such as the market.

Some will argue that the idea of the market as a kind of person with the capacity of speech is an insignificant turn of phrase. Others will excuse it as an innocent figure of speech through which the complexities of the economy can be made comprehensible to a broad audience. For others, this kind of speech will provide firm evidence that our masters are delusional, speaking in twisted and irrational ways. Against each of these positions, I will seek to establish firstly that the prosopopoeia and personification of the market are neither irrelevant nor innocent. Equally, I will argue this figure of speech is not purely false, and when taken seriously can expose some important truths about the ideological symbolisation of the market and beyond this of the place and the function of the market today.

I will therefore propose that the idea that the market might speak is not be dismissed out of hand as a mere illusion. If it is possible to account for something of the symbolic structure of the world in which we are all today invited to live, then this goes beyond the judgement that such manners of speaking are true or false. More socially and politically important is to notice how and why people at a particular point in time might have imagined that something like the market was something that was imagined to have the attributes of speech and personhood. Through the analysis of ideas such as this that may appear trivial, innocent or false it is possible to expose truths about our present predicament.

The task of criticism is, as always, to unearth the presuppositions that lie behind the presentation of things. This task is made difficult when the thing that lies behind appearance is an abstraction. Scrutiny of the idea of the market will reveal that behind the category 'the market' lies abstraction upon abstraction. Behind the idea that the market could speak is the abstract idea that speaking involves intentionality. As will be seen, behind this abstraction rests a series of further abstractions regarding agency and about wishing for inexpressible things. Behind these are abstractions regarding presence and absence, condensation and disappearance, and the coding of speech as speech. To pursue these abstractions is the task of this book, which is done not for the sake of intellectual curiosity but because abstraction is the object of the investigation.

This is so because the market is not an immediately solid body but an abstraction. Its outward manifestations are the materialisation of abstractions. More generally, it should be stressed that to live today is to live amongst abstractions, the origins of which

4

are often obscure and the means by which they could be shrugged off are unclear, even if their power to reorder our lives is painfully apparent. This does not mean that abstraction cannot be contested. It is against these abstractions that others can be invented. As Marx stressed, 'in the analysis of economic forms neither microscopes nor chemical reagents are of assistance. The power of abstraction must replace both'.[3]

Economic categories such as the market and finance present the most pressing philosophical problems of our age. This is because real historical processes, central amongst which is the rise of the market, have created an array of abstractions and have transformed the nature of what is. This real process has resulted in a profound transformation at the ontological level, at the level of what is. As a result of economic, political and cultural changes, there has been an almost complete reversal of the previously held place of the concrete and the abstract. A set of abstractions have risen to centre stage in economic, political and cultural life and among these one abstraction in particular, the abstraction that is 'the market'. The market has become a reality unto itself, at the same time that human bodies and the very existence of the material world have become increasingly incidental when faced with the market.

This is the sense in which the market today 'is' a 'thing', and a thing of utmost importance. The market presents a clear case of the materiality of the spiritual. The market manifests something that Hegel identified more than two centuries ago when he noted how in the course of history, the ways in which an age understands itself, which are externalised in cultural images and fantasies, can become a real active force. We live today amongst abstractions that have taken on the form of things, at the same time that things can appear as mere abstractions. Today Hegel has quite literally been confirmed, such that today spirit *is*, spirit exists, it steps forward in the form of objective reality. Spirit, culture, the realm of the most apparently abstract, has become a real active force, with a concrete sense of material reality. Today it can truly be said, with Hegel, that *'the being of spirit is a bone'*.[4]

These are some of the reasons why accounting for capitalism today requires confronting both its brutally physical presence and equally the 'spirit of capitalism' that accompanies it. It should be stressed, though, that the spirit of capitalism is not a capacity that rests in particular individuals. When Max Weber wrote of the spirit of capitalism, and when such notions recur today, there is often a sense that capitalism involves a particular ethos or sense of personhood that is principally embedded in individuals. The central issue here is not the force of 'psychological sanction' or the logics of justification deployed by individuals, but rather the kinds of symbolic forces that manifest themselves in figures such as the market.[5]

Many have oriented themselves to global economic changes since the 1970s by speaking of neoliberalism, a process through which capitalism secured a reorganisation of economy and politics. To this must be added that during this same period there has been an often unregistered transformation in the cultural criteria by which the function and purpose of economy and politics are understood. As Randy Martin puts it, political economy and cultural economy form the 'twin towers' of the current situation, that of finance ascendant.[6] The reminder is that capitalism involves both bloody expropriation and also ideas, fantasies and abstractions that exceed reason. We do not live in a 'spiritless' age or in a time in which the market has been separated from society. Rather, we are surrounded by the deepest and most outlandish fantasies and the most abstract notions. Capitalism is not purely an economic and political matter but is a cultural and ideational force. Yes, capitalism is bloody, but at the same time circulates in the fantastic and the abstract.

Although the prosopopoeia and personification of the market present a task of social, political, cultural and historical understanding, this book is above all a work of philosophy. Here I seek to comprehend and critically analyse the structure of the ideas and fantasies that come with the category of the market. As always, philosophy is today again threatened, not just by those who would reduce it to logic but equally by the conclusion that holds that reflective thought is not particularly useful. Indeed, if one were to apply the criteria of the market to philosophy then clearly philosophy will never deliver returns. But philosophy always promises to bite back, here by clarifying the remarkable oddity and indeed perversity of the idea that the market could speak. Here we have the edge – even if in the end the market cannot think, at least we can think the market.

2

The market speaks

On 20 September 2011 Olivier Blanchard, Chief Economist at the International Monetary Fund, warned that the global economy had entered a 'dangerous new phase'. Racked by a global financial crisis that had become a sovereign debt crisis, radical measures were proposed for deposing national governments and for instituting austerity measures and structural adjustment across the globe. Blanchard faced the international media and explained what was happening and why radical reforms were required: 'What has happened is that markets have become more skeptical about the ability of policy makers, of governments, to stabilise their public debt'.[7]

The markets have apparently been having doubts about democratically elected governments for some time. In 2011 the elected leaders of Greece and then Italy were ousted so that, as it was explained at the time, it would be possible to respond to the concerns of the markets. It seems that the markets were worried, for instance, that a referendum of the people of Greece might come to the wrong conclusion. As it was put at the time in *The Economist*, 'The markets first welcomed, then worried about the appointment of academic economists as prime ministers of Greece and Italy'.[8]

This direct implication of the market in politics is far from new and is not restricted to the most recent economic and political restructuring. This was seen directly in May 2010, for instance, when the London International Financial Futures and Options Exchange (LIFFE) opened at 1.00am on the night of the UK election for a special session of trading so that the markets could give an early verdict on the results of the election. This intrusion is if anything becoming more apparent today in its audacity and in the depth and breadth of actions that appeals to the market have served to justify.

To understand the political consequences of such practices requires understanding their operation in the sphere of language and the ideas on which they draw. Scrutiny of this language exposes not only that such ways of talking about the market and markets are remarkably widespread, but that they are deeply embedded in a long history, which often rests beneath appearances although at the same time is crucial to the success of such language. To critically comprehend what it means to imagine that the market can be sceptical, anxious or worried about our actions requires a project of social and cultural history, as well as attending to the philosophical challenges presented by prosopopoeia and personification.

Most are quite familiar with clichés in which either a part of the market or the market as a whole is given human characteristics such as speech. 'Money talks', it is said, and 'When Wall Street sneezes, the rest of the world gets a cold'. The market follows a 'random walk', and likewise it is said that 'The market has only two emotions: fear and greed'. Popular guides to investors tell us to 'listen to the market and it will tell you what to do', and one can 'listen to the market and beat the odds'.[9] It is possible to visit websites such as 'The Market Oracle' and investment advisors tell us: 'Believe no one! Listen to what the market is telling you!'.[10]

The prosopopoeia and personification of the market or aspects of the market has a long history. In Greek mythology trade and commerce were personified in the Goddess Tyche. Later, for the Romans, Tyche became Fortuna, a figure who recurs repeatedly throughout history, appearing again, for instance, on the front cover of the first issue of *Fortune* magazine in February 1930.

Consistent with the representation of Tyche and Fortuna, the market, and also finance and credit, are historically personified in a range of forms, often as a woman. In the early eighteenth century Daniel Defoe personified the credit market in the character of Lady Credit, the 'younger sister of money'.[11] In one classic guide to investors from 1933, the credit markets appear in the form of the character 'Cynthia Speculation', who is 'the most alluring of all the children' of Uncle Sam. Here appears a character named 'Cyn':

> She was a vampire incarnate and she led more people astray than the Pied Piper led children. Yet, when she was in her prime, she was so beautiful that no one could resist her. Of charm she had an abundance and she made it known that her admirers need never work. She was devilishly intelligent and yet she could never have exercised her charm and lure had she not had at her command a superabundance of credit. It was only when credit was taken from her that she appeared in her true colors. Then it was found that her eyes were hard, her lips cruel, and her body a mere empty shell.[12]

A similar feminisation of the market can be found in Georg Goodman's guide to playing 'the money game' published in the late 1960s. Here it is written that 'The market is a crowd, and…a crowd of men acts like a single woman. The mind of a crowd is like a woman's mind.'[13] Such speculation makes the frequent association between the market and the apparent irrationality of crowd behaviour, which are then both reduced to the imagined irrationality of a single woman. Thus what Urs Stäheli has critically described as an astonishing chain of equivalence: 'individual male actors = crowd = market = woman'.[14]

Such examples might serve to establish the deeply embedded nature of the personification of the market. Of this personification, two things should be noted immediately. First, the market is personified in a remarkably wide variety of ways, often with what appear quite different purposes. The speech and sentiments attributed to the market appear in a remarkable variety of forms. They appear quite differently in the talk of traders, in television, radio and press media, in literary fiction and film, in the discourses of regulatory bodies, national governments and non-governmental organizations and in academic representations in finance, economics and political economy. These differences are crucial, and these differences in the way that it is claimed or implied that the market can speak or is some kind of person should not be flattened out.

Second, the personification of the market is typically done in such a way that it is unclear as to whether it is intended to be taken literally. Personifications of the market are often taken as self-conscious fabrications. Such is done by the invention of richly figurative characters that represent aspects of market life. Marx for example deploys a complex and generally self-conscious strategy of personification. This happens when, for instance, capital is given the power of speech in order to respond to the question 'what is a working day?', and when he asks 'if commodities could speak', what they would say.[15] Such awareness of the limits of personification is hardly surprising for a thinker for whom individuals are dealt with 'only insofar as they are the personifications of economic categories, the bearers of class-relations and interests'.[16] In such a procedure immediate or concrete figures are used to symbolise structural dynamics, in a way that particular individuals are used to represent something beyond the individual in question.

Michael Hardt and Antonio Negri offer another contemporary example of explicitly self-conscious personification. In their book *Commonwealth* they tell a parable in which Monsieur le Capital feels ill and so presents himself to Doctor Subtilis complaining of bad dreams. In his dream Monsieur le Capital encounters a tree full of ripe fruit and being hungry seizes one of the fruit but finds it is in fact a withered human head. Given that Monsieur le Capital is seeking to seize nothing but subjectivity itself, the core of human being and the basis of certain forms of labour today, Doctor Subtilis advises the cure – that Monsieur le Capital not touch the fruit.[17]

In their use of this fable, Hardt and Negri follow Marx in emphasising that it is misleading to speak of capital as a subject with an interior emotional life. Indeed, their fable exaggerates the improbability of the figures, and the authors are clear that personification is analytically unreliable. While in Marx and in Hardt and Negri the fabulous nature of the personification of the market is absolutely explicit, it must be stressed that most if not all personifications of the market are more or less self-conscious about the imaginary nature of the characterisation. This is a figure of speech that presents itself as such, and in doing so attempts to deflect potential criticism by asserting its status as merely a figure of speech.

This presents a challenge for the critic. Any critique of the personification of the market will achieve little if it simply points to the illusory nature of personification. Most personifications already acknowledge this, at one level or another. To take up the most obvious route of criticism by pointing out that personification is an illusion involves unlocking a door that is already unlocked. This is not an illusion behind which a simple secret is hidden. The market analyst, the politician or the Marxist who represents the market as if it were speaking has an already planned escape route, which allows one to personify the market and give it the power of speech, but if called to account this particular manner of speaking can be excused as being nothing more than a figure of speech.

Such a ploy should not excuse such language. There are many ways to represent complex realities, and putting them in the form of fables is only one strategy. The question is why such fables are effective and what they do, quite apart from the question of how they are intended. In fact, the intentions behind these practices and others are not nearly so important as might be thought. What is important is the operation, the functioning and political consequences of these practices of the attribution of speech and personhood. What is important is to understand why such figures of speech and their associated symbolism work and what they do.

One reason this symbolism is so effective is because it draws on deeply rooted symbolic structures that are part of the history of the West. This includes ideas that are generally taken for granted regarding personhood and the kind of agency that is assumed to rest behind speech. Behind the most directly obvious appearance of the prosopopoeia and personification of the market are a set of social, cultural and historical antecedents. These antecedents will need to be taken into account, as will the conceptual grounds of the figure of prosopopoeia.

The next three chapters will therefore outline three different critiques of the prosopopoeia of the market. In turn these will draw out the desires that rest behind the invention of persons, the quite different ideas of personhood that accompany personification and the theological grounds of the prosopopoeia of the market. This sketch of the dynamics of the prosopopoeia of the market will provide the grounds for the second half of the book, which will ask what this prosopopoeia does and what can be done about it.

3

What do you want?

One might imagine that all reasonable people know that hearing voices is a sign of some form of delusion if not madness. Auditory hallucinations are the most common form of hallucinations, and are identified by the American Psychiatric Association (APA) as a key symptom in the diagnosis of serious psychotic disorders such as schizophrenia. The *Diagnostic and Statistical Manual of Mental Disorders* published by the APA is one of the principal sources for the diagnosis of mental disorders and treats reports of the hearing of voices very seriously. Hearing voices, as with other forms of auditory hallucination, involves experiencing 'A sensory perception that has the compelling sense of reality of a true perception but that occurs without external stimulation of the relevant sensory organ'.[18]

It might appear that the widely reported speech of the market would provide something of a boost for the psychiatric industry. Taken literally, the idea that one can hear the market speak presents precisely as a psychotic symptom. Of course it is hardly original to accuse those in power of madness. When Keynes criticised ostensibly practical men for taking themselves to be free from intellectual influences, he described them as 'Madmen in authority, who hear voices in the air'.[19] The issue is whether it is madness to hear the market speak, and if so then what kind of madness this might be.

In his fine book on voice, Jonathan Rée argues that 'there is no sector of our vocabularies which is so uninhibited and extravagant, or so open to popular improvisation and inventiveness, as that which represents the world of sound'. Rée notes how auditory hallucinations take advantage of the 'peculiar unarguability of the experience of hearing'. Impressions based on things claimed to have been seen can be checked against the evidence while sounds and voices pass in time and are restricted in space and so are not available for the same processes of verification. One can always insist that the reported voice heard really spoke, with the alibi that others missed it or were not there at the right moment.

> If your first visual impressions do not tally with your later investigations, they can be discounted and attributed to your imagination instead. But sounds are not amenable to that kind of reality-testing and cross-checking, since they do not make any such definite claims to spatial location. If you think you hear something strange – your whispered name as you stand alone in a susurrating wood, or footsteps in a deserted house – you have no reliable way of reassuring yourself that it was only an illusion.[20]

Beyond the complex matter of evidence is the fact of the remarkably widespread nature of reports of hearing voices. There is a long history of hearing voices, in figures such as Socrates, Jesus and Jean of Arc. There is also a long veneration of oracles and witnesses, those who hear and are inspired by mysterious voices that only they can hear.[21]

Further, there are a range of entities that are treated as if they speak, with a diverse range of functions and purposes. When given the power of speech, a horse such as Black Beauty can speak directly to us, and another such as Mister Ed can speak to his master. In such personifications, animals are given character-istics usually preserved for humans, in a way that invites empathy or humour. In the yoghurt advertisement that invites the viewer to 'listen to your gut', there is an appeal to the idea of listening to one's body, in which such listening involves as a result listening to the instruction to purchase a product. A few years ago the National Aeronautics and Space Administration agency (NASA) released recordings from space, in which it was said that one could hear stars and planets singing.

These cultural orientations indicate the widespread nature of prosopopoeia and the diverse uses to which it is put. They illustrate something of the depth of the cultural practice of prosopopoeia, and also recall one of the starting points of this analysis, which is that the attribution of speech to entities not usually considered able to speak brings with it more than the power of speech. Prosopopoeia invests the target with a spirit, a will and an interior, whether this is to encourage empathy for animals, to invite spectators to laugh, to purchase a product or to marvel at the universe.

To clarify this question of what prosopopoeia brings with it, the case of Daniel Paul Schreber is illustrative. Schreber is a classic case of someone troubled by the hearing of voices, and is also an important case in discussions in psychoanalysis of paranoid delusion and psychosis. His case can illuminate what can be called the *psychoanalytic critique of the prosopopoeia of the market*, which will offer important armoury in scrutinising the idea that the market might be able to speak. This particular critique will move beyond dismissal of prosopopoeia towards asking what motivates the attribution of speech.

Schreber suffered from what would today be identified as schizophrenia, and he certainly experienced sensations that others would not be likely to sense. He heard ticks and bangs, and voices both babbling and coherent. These voices posed Schreber with a quite practical problem, not merely of how to deal with their frustrating distraction but as to what they meant. Schreber created an entire explanation of reality in which he could explain the voices. In the memoirs of his nervous illness, published in 1903, Schreber explained that just as humans are composed of nerves, so God is a manifestation of a complex set of invisible rays. The world has however fallen from grace, which is why the rays communicate complex messages to him. Schreber was governed by one particular instruction, in that he needed to become a woman in order to copulate with God. This was necessary because all people on earth had died or would soon die, and the voices told him that sexual relations with God were required for the continuation of human life on earth.[22]

In Freud's reading of this case, published in 1911, Schreber's nervous disorder was a result of a sublimated desire, a desire for a socially inexpressible object. His wish to become a woman for the purposes of copulation were the expression in a roundabout way of his homosexual desires for his father, which he could not express socially but nevertheless found their way into his consciousness. In projecting his desires outside of himself, Schreber was able to say something that he was otherwise not permitted to say.[23]

Freud's reading is highly selective in its conclusions and is premised on a set of assumptions that are hard to maintain, but what Freud draws attention to in his reading of Schreber is the way that apparently irrational delusions can have their origin in the effort to express otherwise inexpressible desires. Indeed, what Freud's reading of Schreber offers, which is one of the enduring insights of psychoanalysis, is the presentation of the question of what it is, despite what might be said, someone actually wants. Faced with social interdictions regarding what can legitimately be said, things are often said in a roundabout kind of way.

Schreber's case presents a situation of projection or sublimation, a matter of shifting objects of desire from one place to another. In the case of Schreber there is an elevation of one's father to the place of the sun, from which rays emanate. With the construction of the market as a subject there is equally a raising up of market relationships into that of an imagined external agent with special powers. Along with this projection comes the frustrating unattainability of that object of desire, the delusion that strengthens with the idea of the supersensual nature of that object. The market is something beyond what anyone could possibly contain or control.

These projective elevations are not just signs of madness. They can be found just as much in dreams, fantasies and the creations of the imaginary. The delusion, as with a dream or fantasy, is a sign or a marker of a desire. In his *Interpretations of Dreams*, Freud introduces the idea that dreams are the fulfilment of a wish.

Dreams...are not meaningless, they are not absurd; they do not imply that one portion of our store of ideas is asleep while another portion is beginning to wake. On the contrary, they are psychical phenomena of complete validity – fulfilments of wishes; they can be inserted into the chain of intelligible waking mental acts; they are constructed by a highly complicated activity of the mind.[24]

The fantastic figure of our imagination then stands in for something other than itself. It is indeed the distance between Schreber and the object of his desire that is important. Similarly, when it is said that the market is like this or that, that the market wants this or that, the psychoanalytic question is: what does the one who says this want? The projected imaginary object 'the market' that is invested with all manner of characteristics is the function of an externalised desire. Located in the other, speaking as the voice of the other, I do not need to say what I want. The external object that is 'the market' is therefore a perfect alibi. It is not me who wants these things. I am merely giving voice to the desires of an external other.

Such a position provides a powerful critical location from which to dissect statements about what the market 'wants'. To the investment banker who explains what the markets want, or the political agency that seeks to restructure an economy in order to reassure the markets, the psychoanalytic question is thus radically disarming – 'I can hear very well what you say that the markets want, but when you are saying that the markets want this, what do you want?'.

Further complexity can be added to the psychoanalytic critique of the prosopopoeia of the market in light of the later interpretation of Schreber that appears in the teachings of Jacques Lacan. Lacan takes up the case of Schreber in his third seminar, his seminar on the psychoses. What is important here is the emphasis that Lacan puts on the place of language in paranoid delusion. Indeed, he places the dislocation of speech and the question 'Who speaks?' at the centre of his treatment of psychosis. This is far from arbitrary, as is already intimated with the close association between hearing voices and madness, and also the displacements of desire noted by Freud. What Lacan adds is a recognition of the way that psychosis involves a discon- nection between a subject and the symbolic order. Thus, Lacan stresses to his students that 'for us to have a psychosis, there must be disturbances of language'.

In this seminar on the psychoses Lacan introduces his concept of 'the name of the father'. This does not refer to a natural father or a particular or specifically male figure but rather to an ordering principle, the 'order that prevents the collision and explosion of the situation'.[25] In what is known as 'normal' human functioning, a subject is able to secure themselves against the name of the father, which provides consistency and a semblance of order. As symbolic animals we are all hearing voices all the time. The psychotic hears voices in breach of what is recognised as existing within the symbolic order.

While hallucination is related to an experienced or imagined sensory stimulation 'without external stimulation of the relevant sensory organ', the *Diagnostic and Statistical Manual of Mental Disorders* is of little assistance when it comes to the prosopopoeia of the market. In the apparent psychosis of those who say that the market can speak, it emerges that the sounds of the market do not occur in the absence of external stimulation of the sensory organs. Indeed, participation in markets often involves a radical *overstimulation* of the senses. It is not that the market does not surround us with sounds, but rather what to do with these sounds and how to understand what it means to listen to them.

If this is not madness, then it is a particular torsion in the structure of language. This is not so much something to do with the peculiarities of particular minds, but with peculiarities of imagining and speaking. This offers an important addition or clarification to the psychoanalytic critique of the prosopopoeia of the market – to say that the market can speak is not madness but rather reflects a peculiarity if not a psychosis of language. It is not necessarily a twisting of the subject so much as a contortion of language. To say that the market can speak would then not be a sign of individual psychosis. To say or to allow it to be said that something like the market can speak is therefore what is known as *folie à deux*, a shared or collective psychosis in which two or more share a common delusion. To imagine that something like the market is a kind of person that has a will, intentions and might speak is not an individual pathology. It is rather a shared psychosis, in which the market is made the placeholder of desires and an ordering regulator, that is, the market comes to stand in the place of the name of the father.

4

What kind of person?

The attribution of speech and personhood to the market might seem to involve a simple substitution, in which characteristics that belong to human beings are attributed to non-human entities. The prosopopoeia of the market would then involve an imaginary displacement or projection of human speech onto the market. The personification of the market would involve an additional attribution of sentiment and will. This process in combination would involve finding in an abstract entity attributes that are properly and uniquely human characteristics. It will emerge, however, that things are not so simple as they might seem. To understand the prosopopoeia and personification of the market will require entering into complex questions regarding the broader significance of the giving of voice to beings that are generally considered unable to speak.

Personification rests on the idea that there is something specifically human that justifies claims to personhood. This is generally overlooked in the apparent obviousness that 'a person is a person'. In fact, personification involves first of all the identification of quite specific aspects of humans and concluding that these are what persons are or that these are possessed only by people. The difficulty lies in this first step, in which particular characteristics are assumed to be properly human.

To adapt a concept from political economy, it can be said that personification, which involves the idea that a person is uniquely a person, involves a generally hidden previous process that can be called primary personification. This is a long historical process by which the idea of the person was invented, which involves the reality of the personification of people. That this primary personification is generally hidden becomes apparent upon critical scrutiny. It makes no sense to speak of the personification of the planets, nature or any other thing, without at least some rudimentary prior idea of what it means to be a person.

The idea of the person and of personhood developed through a complex and constantly contested historical process. The history of the production of the modern person or 'the individual' is relatively well known, in part due to the work by Michel Foucault, which excavated this history of the invention of the modern conception of 'man'.[26] What is important to add is that the invention of persons involves much more than the invention of the personhood of persons. The concept of the person has not been simply restricted to people, but rather has subsequently been taken to belong to people and also to other entities. The process of primary personification lies in the background when non-human things or animals are credited with human attributes. When certain animals are selected as possessing human attributes, this is not just a selection amongst the animals but a selection amongst which human characteristics will be used as the basis of comparison. In the background of such processes rests this primary personification and with it a particular idea of what counts as a person.

This practice of transferring something from the human or 'man' (anthrōpos) onto something non-human is often called anthropomorphism. One crucial manifestation of anthropomorphism appears in the attribution of human characteristics to nature. A remarkable range of cultures have the idea of the natural environment as being composed of physical things or forces which are taken to have personhood. Many cultures identify earth as mother and sky as father, or identify the moon and planets with particular persons. The planet Jupiter is taken not simply as a lump of matter but is given human characteristics and is presented as in some ways something akin to a person. As the god of war, Jupiter can then exaggerate those aspects of the human that are projected onto this figure that is then taken as

'Jupiter'.

Personification is not just done to lumps of matter, but to abstract notions. Abstract concepts such as luck, wisdom or justice have at various points in time been localised in something that appears as a bounded physical body, sometimes given permanence by for instance being carved in stone and given social significance by being placed in prominent social spaces. Personification involves more than simply attributing human characteristics to non-human entities. It is selective, and can attribute characteristics that exceed any actually existing person. Personification also involves the attribution of superhuman powers or abstract notions to objects. The invention of persons involves personification but beyond this also processes of the attribution of abstract powers. These powers can be human or 'more than human', the powers of deities in what is known as deification.

There are many ideas of what a person is or could be, maybe even an infinite number. For this reason, the basic critical question with respect to any personification is to ask what kind of person is the personified object imagined to be. Following on from the psychoanalytic critique of prosopopoeia considered in the previous chapter, it is therefore possible to identify a second critique, which can be called the *critique of the primary personification of the market*. When the market is taken as a kind of person, this critique asks what kind of person it is taken to be. The critique of the primary personification of the market will be the basis for the analysis of the voice of the market in the next chapter, but first some preliminaries are required regarding the relation of personification and prosopopoeia and the difficult question of whether or not prosopopoeia is avoidable or necessarily negative.

The critique of the primary personification of the market is given some specificity and bite by focusing on the specific aspect of prosopopoeia. Focusing on one particular aspect of personification, that is, the processes of the attribution of voice and speech, gives a way of being concrete in the analysis of the kinds of personhood that are attributed to the market. As has been argued, the giving of voice to non-human entities generally involves a matter of conferring personhood, and with this the nobility that comes with personhood in a culture that honours the dignity of the person. Giving voice involves giving more than the capacity for mechanically reproducing speech. When voice is given to something that was imagined not to have it, this involves a valuation, and an attribution of meaningful intention and the demand that that agent be heard.

Prosopopoeia involves finding personhood or face (*prosōpon*) where none is expected. In the figure of prosopopoeia an imagined or absent person is given the powers of personhood, presence and speech. The classic conception of prosopopoeia is found in the first century Roman rhetorician Quintilian, for whom prosopopoeia and impersonation involves masking the origins of speech. Quintilian marvels at the effectiveness of these figures, considering them to have greater force than for example *parrhēsia*, the critical intervention of speaking truth. The figures of impersonation or prosopopoeia are bolder, he says, and require 'stronger lungs'. Moreover, he writes:

> These both vary and animate a speech to a remarkable degree. We use them (1) to display the inner thoughts of our opponents as though they were talking to themselves (but they are credible only if we imagine them saying what it is not absurd for them to have thought!), (2) to introduce conversations between ourselves and others, or of others among themselves, in a credible manner, and (3) to provide appropriate characters for words of advice, reproach, complaint, praise or pity. We are even allowed in this form of speech to bring down the gods from heaven or raise the dead; cities and nations even acquire a voice.[27]

24

Following Aristotle in finding speech only in humans, Quintilian specifies that 'we cannot of course imagine speech except as speech of a person'.[28] This is the tradition that as was noted earlier runs through Spinoza to the present day, in which speech and personhood are bound intimately to one another. Thus in the middle of the nineteenth century John Ruskin would object to the way that human sentiments and pathos were so widely and cheaply given to things which could not possibly possess them. In doing so he identified what he called the 'pathetic fallacy', the mistake of finding pathos where there is none. Ruskin was thus savagely critical of poets such as Coleridge. In his poem 'Christabel', Coleridge writes:

> There is not enough wind to twirl
> The one red leaf, the last of its clan
> That dances as often as dance it can,
> Hanging so light, and hanging so high,
> On the topmost twig that looks at the sky.[29]

Ruskin objects that the leaf is here given a capacity that only human beings possess, that of dancing. Perhaps most importantly, Coleridge attributes intentionality to the leaf when it has none, as if the leaf had consciousness and will. Ruskin argues that in such figurative language Coleridge

> has a morbid, that is to say, a so far false, idea about the leaf: he fancies a life in it, and will, which there are not; confuses its powerlessness with choice, its fading death with merriment, and the wind that shakes it with music. The temperament which admits the pathetic fallacy, is, as I said above, that of a mind and body in some sort too weak to deal fully with what is before them or upon them.[30]

Following such a line of thinking, it could be argued that the personification and prosopopoeia of the market reflect the pathetic fallacy exactly. To say that the market can speak, that it could be sceptical or disappointed, that it would be angry or uncertain, would be false if not morbid. Further, with Ruskin, one might say that this reflects a weakness of mind that refuses to deal fully with the reality of what the market is. To say that the market speaks would thus be one of the most vulgar and simple-minded reductions of a complex reality into a single person with a voice and will.

The question that remains, however, is whether prosopopoeia is a mistake and if the attribution of pathos to non-human entities is only and always a fallacy. To begin with, it should be recognised that the very act of using proper nouns, which happens for instance when children are given names, also involves the giving of personhood and face to a subject that can be absent. Proper nouns, which give names to people and places, operate exactly so that it is possible to give presence when bodies are otherwise absent.

Taking such recognition seriously, Paul de Man argues that prosopopoeia, far from being an avoidable illusion, is part of what he calls 'the madness of words'. This can be seen quite clearly in the practice of reading. Whether reading silently or aloud, the act of reading is precisely one of giving voice or face to an absent author. In reading, voice is given to at least one absent subject, the author, and is also given to a range of other characters. This is not simply an illusion or a mistake, but is part of the wonder of participation in language. Thus, de Man argues:

> to read is to understand, to question, to know, to forget, to erase, to deface, to repeat – that is to say, the endless prosopopoeia by which the dead are made to have a face and a voice which tells the allegory of their demise and allows us to apostrophize them in our turn. No degree of knowledge can ever stop this madness, for it is the madness of words.[31]

It might be, then, that acts of the substitution of voice and speech are far less unusual than is often thought. Ventriloquism, the giving of breath or voice to an object not apparently possessed of it, is in this sense not such an uncommon act. Indeed, this is what reading aloud is – bringing into presence an author absent or dead. Thus personification and prosopopoeia are perhaps as old as our languages themselves. In language, we are surrounded by such figures, which is part of the reason that it is hard to notice them. We constantly apostrophise these figures into which we impute the capacity of speech.

Another problem which threatens to derail any attempt to criticise prosopopoeia or the pathetic fallacy is, as has been noted, that the person is as much an invention as any other creation. This is the problem drawn out by the concept of primary personification, in that it stresses the way that the imagination that there is a particular kind of thing called the person which is in possession of uniquely human capacities is the result of a prior operation that is so often forgotten. The person may well be the most remarkable of human inventions, the most elaborate and astonishing fabrication of human artifice. What are called persons are the result of this personification, just as what are called subjects are the outcome of a process of 'subjectification'. The issue is not just that it is false to think that a subject like the market is made up, while on the other hand there are real human subjects that are not invented.

The fact that there are only invented persons means that it is possible to struggle to reinvent ourselves and our inventions. The psychoanalytic critique of the prosopopoeia of the market, outlined in the previous chapter, identified how these invented figures can express desires, dreams or fantasies, and these expressions are partial and subjected to expectations about what can be legitimately expressed. These inventions are neither unchangeable nor politically innocent and something significant about the cultural politics of an age can be seen in which entities

27

are held or imagined to be subjects and which are considered able to speak.

Transformations in this cultural politics invite reconfigurations of the giving of personhood and voice. This can involve attempts to silence certain voices, or can involve seeking to speak for those who are silenced and giving voice to those who have none. In the Old Testament the injunction appears: 'Speak up for those who cannot speak for themselves, for the rights of all who are destitute' (Prov. 31: 8). The cultural politics of prosopopoeia are at the heart of the political work of those who struggle for the rights of people, animals, and a planet that cannot speak. When it is said that Mother Earth is weeping at what we have done, that children have rights even if they cannot express them, or if one senses real anguish behind the cries of a suffering animal, then there is a process of giving voice and spirit in a context in which there is otherwise thought to be none.

These are some of the reasons why prosopopoeia and person-ification are if not unavoidable then not universally or simply negative. This is further reason as to why the goal with respect to the speaking market might not then be simply to root it out as a fallacy. Given their deeply embedded nature and their varying purposes and functions, it might be better to put aside judgement about what is really a subject and where speech really issues from. This might make it possible to consider more carefully the depth of this thought and exactly why it is so hard to stamp it out.

To this end it is possible to find useful methodological guidance in Foucault's important discussion of the dynamics of the invention of the figure of the author. Here Foucault proposes to abandon the old questions such as 'Who is the real author?', a question that he calls 'tiresome'. Instead, he presents the following questions with which one can interrogate instances of speech:

What are the modes of existence of this discourse?

Where does it come from; how is it circulated; who controls it?

What placements are determined for possible subjects?[32]

Rather than thinking that speech has one true and proper location and that the task is to find it only there and to police it back into its place, the insistence is that there is speech and it surrounds and invades us all. The question of the market speaking is then not so much moralism about speech properly belonging to humans but rather one of the functioning and operation of that speech, how that speech works and what it does.

The prosopopoeia of the market is not madness and neither is it a mistake. Rather than seek to discredit or dismiss it, the problem is the mode of existence and circulation of this discourse and the placements of subjects in this discourse. The psychoanalytic critique of prosopopoeia developed in the previous chapter drew attention to the question of the displacement of desire that can operate behind speech. The critique of the primary personification of the market developed here enables one to ask, when it is said that the market can speak, what kind of person it is that is speaking.

5

The voice and will of God

When it is said that the market speaks, this speech tends to involve something more than one would expect of any mere mortal. The prosopopoeia of the market involves more than a simple anthropomorphism or personification in which human capacities are attributed to the market. Sometimes the market seems perfectly human, but it is also not uncommon to find the market given great powers that exceed those that are thought to belong to human beings. The range and capacity of powers that have been attributed to the market leads to the idea that there is a quite different metaphorical substitution at play. Instead of the market looking like a human being, the market takes on super-human form. In terms of the status and reverence if not adulation of the market today, one is lead therefore to see the way that the market is treated in ways that are otherwise reserved for the gods or for God.

Such a recognition is the basis of the kind of claim found in discussions of the market as God, or in discussions of capitalism or economics as involving religious or theological grounds.[33] This is also what lies behind a range of popular criticisms of the adulation of the market. This can be seen, for example, in the episode of South Park that lampoons the idea that there is a need to obey the economy. In this episode Randy Marsh preaches an obviously recognisable parody of the way that the economy has taken on the character of God:

We have become lovers of pleasure rather than lovers of the Economy! There are those who will say that the Economy has forsaken us. Nay. You have forsaken the Economy! And now you know the Economy's wrath. O thou'st can shop at a

sporting goods store, but knowest thou that the Economy will
take away thy Bronco's cap from thine head! Mock the
Economy without fear? Thine own stockbrokers now lie dead
by their own hand and thou knowest that thy stockbrokers
did not fear the Economy! Well here we are, my friends. You
have brought the Economy's vengeance upon yourselves![34]

This kind of parody is typically based on the idea that it is
strange to find religious thinking in the sphere of something like
the market, which is supposed to be predicated on the cold calcu-
lation of individual gain. There is of course a long tradition that
has sought to understand the continuities between economics
and religion, and this tradition shows that it is not at all strange
to find religious ideas in the economic sphere. Marx frequently
attacked political economists for treating capitalism in much the
same way that theologians treated God. Carl Schmitt famously
argued that 'All significant concepts of the modern state are
secularised theological concepts'.[35] Following this line of
thinking, which is alive and well today, it is not unusual or
strange to note that belief in the market is a matter of faith, that
economics is the scripture presented to the faithful, and that the
figure at the centre of this faith is the market.

Following the psychoanalytic critique of the prosopopoeia of
the market and the critique of the primary personification of the
market outlined in the previous two chapters, it is therefore
possible to identify a third critique of the prosopopoeia and
personification of the market, which can be called the *theological
critique of the prosopopoeia of the market*. This critique elaborates
the religious grounding of the idea that the market can speak but
moreover, by taking up the theological thread it will clarify
important elements in the critique of the primary personification
of the market, by identifying in more concrete detail the specific
kind of person that tends to be speaking in the prosopopoeia of
the market. This chapter will outline this third critique, which

along with the other critiques will offer an outline of the nature of the prosopopoeia of the market. This will provide the basis for the remainder of the book, which will ask what this prosopopoeia of the market does and what can be done about it.

The discovery of theological motifs in secular contexts is central to Nietzsche's critique of the apparent death of God. Nietzsche does not merely assert the death of God in the sense that it might be easy to dispel belief in God as a delusion. Rather, he shows that even with the apparent decline of Christian faith there is a continuous tendency to attribute godlike powers to figures that come to stand in the place of God. God, it would seem, is a deeply embedded notion and has many surrogates. Thus he writes: 'God is dead; but in the way of men, there may still be caves for thousands of years in which his shadow will be shown. And we – we still have to vanquish his shadow too'.[36]

Nietzsche argues that the birth of the modern conception of personhood and above all the figure of 'man' rises with the death of God. Stepping away from a deity that is omnipotent and commands us offers a sense of our own powers and our command over ourselves. The modern subject or person with an interiority and command over others arises exactly in this context of emancipation from religious illusion, even though the idea of interiority is in many ways a direct continuation of the Christian tradition. The death of God is therefore not so much a death as a passing over, a transference or a substitution of one imagined subject for another. For Nietzsche this result, this thing called 'man' is a limited and restricted form of what the human could be, and thus something to be overcome.

This line of thinking is extended by Foucault in his history of the modern conception of man. Foucault acknowledges the theological grounds of the modern conception of the person as singular and causal and also that the full and final death of God will require nothing less than what he calls 'the death of man'. And here Nietzsche's critique is taken up directly, stressing that the death of God would require the elimination of the surrogates of God, all of the figures that have been put in the place of God. Moreover, the death of God would not leave man in a place of safety or security. As Foucault puts it, 'What Nietzsche's thought heralds is the death of his murderer'.[37]

Questions remain regarding the extent to which the figure of God was replaced by the figure of man. Nietzsche and Foucault identify an important transition in the substitution of man for God, but this is only part of the story when it comes to the invention of subjects that stand in the place of God. In their almost complete ignorance of economic matters Nietzsche and in particular the early Foucault fail to register that the age of the death of God is not only the age of the birth of man. Modernity may be the age of man but it is also the age of capital. Crucially, this involves a process in which the figures of capitalism come to stand in the place of God. In this light it is hardly surprising to find that the death of God involves not only the rise of man but moreover also the birth of the modern idea of the market.

Although missing in his early work, glimpses of an elaboration of such economic politics appear in Foucault's later lectures on the history of biopolitics. Here Foucault identifies how, in the middle of the eighteenth century, the market became what he calls a 'site of truth'. The market, he argues, became at this time a location of veridiction, of speaking the truth, in which the market as site became a locus not merely for sorting commodities, but equally for sorting statements between the true and the false. As Foucault puts it, at this time, 'the market is becoming what I will call a site of veridiction. The market must tell the truth'.[38]

As with many of Foucault's remarks in his lectures, such a formulation is equivocal and imprecise, even if this imprecision can lead to illuminating insights. It is possible to locate two quite distinct claims here, which lead to very different conclusions. On the one hand there is the idea that in the middle of the eighteenth century the market became a site in which statements are judged to be true or false. Thus within an historical process of the politics of truth, it might be that participants whose statements pass through the market can claim veracity or truthfulness.

On the other hand is the idea that at this time the market itself became the kind of agent that might be capable of telling the truth. This idea is important insofar as the concern here is not with the action of people in markets so much as it is with the idea that the market itself is a kind of person. Moreover, in this context, the idea here is that the market might be a subject who might be able to tell the truth. This raises the thorny question of whether or not the market is the kind of subject known for telling the truth, and with this a series of questions regarding how the market tells this truth and to whom.

Foucault provides a spur that moves beyond the mere coincidence of the market and God that could help to clarify exactly what kind of speech it is that issues from God, and with this the particularities of the divine characteristics that are found when the market speaks. When considering the market as God there is something well beyond the mere status of elevation. There is much more than merely claiming for the market the powers of omniscience or benevolence, in which as with God the market is now taken to know all and to display a universally beneficent hand. While such divine attributes are at times present, attention to prosopopoeia will expose deeper and more subtle continuities between the market and religion. The idea that the market has a voice and a will is a direct instance of the market being taken as God, with a voice and a will. But further still, when the market is taken as God, this generally involves a distinct conception of the nature of God, and a specific conception of speech and willing. Along with this notion of God, it is possible to locate the forms of understanding of what we ourselves are and our powers in relation to this creation that is the market.

As was stressed in the discussion of primary personification, to understand personification requires more than identification of the fact of substitution of one thing for another. It requires consideration of what kind of conception of the person is taken as the starting point of this substitution. In the same way, to understand the projection of the characteristics of God onto the market requires consideration of the question as to exactly what kind of conception of God is being projected onto the market. Here the question of voice provides a vital clue.

Importantly, this God that is the market is rarely an omnipotent God with a clear and booming voice. More often than not this is a mysterious God, one who might well speak the truth but does not speak it directly to all. To understand this voice requires being a member of the elect few, and this is not an election in which human beings vote. The voice of God that is the market produces speech that is elliptical, enigmatic and filled with riddles, even if it is imagined that behind this speech there is supposed to be an intending agent whose intentions are as clear as the rays of the sun. If this is a God that can speak then this is a quite particular God and one that speaks in subtle and amazing ways.

In Biblical texts God often speaks. Although agents are sometimes sent on his behalf to enact his will, at crucial moments God creates great marvels with his voice alone, although this voice remains somehow distant to us as humans. It is thus said, for example, that 'God's voice thunders in marvellous ways; he does great things beyond our understanding' (Job 37:5).

This prosopopoeia presents a specific idea about the way that God speaks. It also makes clear one of the most ancient ideas about speech, that is, the idea that speech is governed by intentions that often surpass specific instances of speech. Intention is crucial because even if speech is incomprehensible it is possible to postulate a meaning that was intended behind apparently mystifying speech or signs. This creates the problem of the mystery of God's intention and with it the problem of meaning, a problem that has puzzled theologians for centuries. Not only is there the problem about what to do with this or that instruction, but equally there is the problem of what is to be done when God is not immediately present and when it is hard or indeed impossible to understand what God has commanded.

6

Divine mumbling

Walter Benjamin tells a story about a chess machine in which it appears that a puppet smoking a hookah pipe plays, while in fact a chess master dwarf hides inside the machine pulling strings that move the puppet's hands. The hands of the dwarf and indeed the dwarf's very existence are hidden from view and so, dissimulating the location of agency, the puppet – or maybe the dwarf – is able to win every time.[39]

The machine in question was first created in 1769 by Wolfgang von Kempelen to entertain the Empress Maria Theresa. This chess machine was not, however, the most prized creation of von Kempelen, who also sought to create a machine that could produce the sounds of human speech. In the same year that he invented the chess machine he created a 'speaking machine' that could produce sounds recognisable as human speech. When he toured Europe displaying his creations, the chess machine was presented as the main act although audiences found the speaking machine much more disconcerting. It was at this time quite surprising to learn that speech could be produced as if out of thin air and in the absence of an animating agent. As Mladen Dolar writes, 'the meaning was hard to decipher, given the poor quality of the reproduction, but the voice was what immediately seized everyone and inspired universal awe'. Dolar reports the surprise that was experienced by listeners to this speaking machine, which exceeded the surprise at seeing a puppet winning at chess.

No matter how much the thing was described for everybody to study, the machine nevertheless kept producing effects which can only be described with the Freudian word 'uncanny'. There is an uncanniness in the gap which enables a machine, by purely mechanical means, to produce something so uniquely human as voice and speech. It is as if the effect could emancipate itself from its mechanical origin, and start functioning as a surplus – indeed, as the ghost in the machine; as if there were an effect without a proper cause, an effect surpassing explicable cause.[40]

Such a machine would hardly be surprising today, given the widespread presence of telecommunication devices by which voices can be conjured up with remarkable ease. In fact, von Kempelen's speaking machine is a precursor of modern speech recording and telephony, and it is in part thanks to him that we are now quite familiar with the idea of voices originating elsewhere than where they are heard. To live today means to be surrounded by devices with which we can secure the presence of the voices of others in spite of their physical absence.

The cultural significance of this surround sound should not be underestimated. This conjuration of sound creates a situation that exceeds the typical ploy of ventriloquism, in which a ventriloquist pretends to not move their lips while a dummy is shown to move theirs. Indeed, the humour that surrounds ventriloquism today is generally based on the self-conscious awareness of the banality and obviousness of the pretence of the dislocation of voice. By contrast, the prosopopoeia of the market involves a fundamental and almost permanent mystery as to which intending subject might lie behind the speech of the market and animate it. There seems to be an animating agency, but it cannot easily be reduced back to any particular agent.

This mystery of intentionality is essential to the operation of the speaking machine that is the market. Here the interweaving of voice and will is fundamental, and in particular the tendency that has been stressed before in which the attribution of voice involves attribution of an intentionality behind speech. This happens even with things that might otherwise be taken merely as 'noise'. Consider for example the device known as the TickTrola, a piece of computer software that quite literally enables one to 'listen to the market'. This is achieved by a sound being played at a particular pitch, which is modulated according to the movement of stockmarket prices so that if the market goes up then the pitch rises and vice versa. One can then listen to the TickTrola either in real time as prices rise and fall or one can play the musical symbolisation of particular moments in the history of the market such as, for example, during market crises.

What is uncanny about the TickTrola is the way this mechanism invites listeners to envisage a composer that might be animating such rises and falls. Here as elsewhere in the symbolisation of the market, it is not hard to see that if one listens to such 'market music', or if one follows the daily logic of such seemingly random processes, in a culture that is so deeply grounded in the idea that speech issues from the intentions of a speaking subject, it is unsurprising that it is thought that the speech, voice or music of something like the market might issue from an intending subject.

The task ahead is to clarify what the prosopopoeia of the market does, and to this end the three critiques outlined so far provide important grounding. Recognising the particular forms of speech of the market and the presupposition of intentionality enables clarification of how this idea of an intending subject does important work in positing an always elusive agency that rests behind observable signs. The interiority of this author manifests itself not as an anonymous mechanism. Rather, the market can be taken to be governed by some manner of designer or mechanic. This is not merely a wheel or a clock that turns by its own motive power, but is rather wound by an invisible agency that has created the marvel. This presupposition of agency is present just as much when the market is taken as God as when one posits the market as the Devil.

Here there is a crucial element in the form of appearance of the prosopopoeia of the market. This intending subject supposedly behind the market almost always appears in the form of a third person. The market does not speak in the first person as 'I'. It does not pop up on the television and explain what it has been thinking and what it wants. Neither does the market present itself in the second person as a 'we'. The market appears as somehow outside any 'us', which comes with the projection of the market as something external. The market invariably takes the form of a third person subject, an 'it' that is speaking.

The speaking market also almost always appears in singular form. Even if one speaks of 'the markets', even this expression is a strange form of singular plural. Although the markets are an agglomeration, a collective of the actions of many, in taking the market as a person and above all as a person capable of speech, this multiplicity is reduced to an agency that can speak with one voice. The prosopopoeia of the market reduces the market or the markets to an 'it' and above all a One.

This invention of an external singularity is accompanied by a specific form of speech behind which lies a deeper intentionality. The attribution of intentionality is important because regardless of what it says, the intentions of the market remain almost always hidden from view. This lack of transparency is vital. If the market speaks the truth then it is a truth that is of necessity hidden. Truth lies not in the surface of this speech but somewhere deeper.

The author of this speech therefore remains a mysterious and ineffable one. This is a form of speech marked by its lightness and its insubstantial nature. This makes it no less effective, but is part of how the prosopopoeia of the market works. Although it is asserted with force that the market intends and speaks, this speech is not a speech of full and pure presence. The attribution of speech to the market is marked by a double movement in which the market is both attributed speech, but this attribution is then supplemented by the idea that the speech of the market takes place elsewhere. The market can speak, but it is mysterious speech in need of deciphering, and this is why it requires others to comprehend its speech and to speak on its behalf.

In these respects the idea that the market can speak is continuous with ancient practices of divination and soothsaying. Such practices are kept alive in popular form today in practices such as Tarot reading, palm reading, fortune telling and astrology. In reading these signs or when listening to the market one takes partial or fragmentary signs as clues to a deeper meaning. Behind such phenomena rests the idea that signs are taken to 'speak' but that they speak enigmatically. They speak the truth but do not speak it directly, and this is why they require a labour of deciphering. What becomes important in such practices are the techniques and apparatuses of decipherment, which are usually conferred legitimacy by a combination of tradition and the assertion of expert command over the material at hand. It is experts alone that can decode the signs and can give their verdict about what the will of the gods or the markets command.

In his analysis of the *Los Angeles Times* astrology column, Theodor Adorno introduced the concept of 'secondary super-stition' to explain the social functions of superstitions such as astrology. Drawing on the sociological concept of primary and secondary groups, which explains the way that influence in complex societies is typically drawn not directly from figures of power but is mediated through representatives of power, Adorno identified the way that astrology is received at one remove. Given that few have the means to afford direct access to professional astrologers, one receives interpretation of astro-logical information from an 'abstract authority' such as the expert analyst in a respectable newspaper. In the encounter of this information 'the mechanics of the astrological system are never divulged and the readers are presented only with the alleged results of astrological reasoning in which the reader does not actively participate'.[41]

If the interpretation of financial markets seems to follow a similar logic, then this is not because these markets are superstitious, but because they follow the logic Adorno describes as involving secondary access to information, absence of access to the mechanism of production of information, and the abstract authority of market analysts. In this abstract authority lies a crucial element of the politics of the prosopopoeia of the market. In his important book on finance Alex Preda has documented the shifting practices of exclusion which 'frame' finance and set boundaries around which groups can claim the right to legitimately know the market. He documents how finance has always involved contestation between various 'status groups' that seek to control access to information about and control over the market.[42] Likewise, Christian Marazzi has identified the way that finance has developed what he calls 'a rather esoteric neolanguage'. As he writes, 'It is thus under the shelter of this linguistic opacity that finance prospers, which raises the question of democracy, that is, the possibility of publicly debating strategies, procedures, and decisions concerning the lives of all citizens'.[43]

What must be stressed here is that the cultural and ideational antecedents to this linguistic opacity are central to the operation of the idea of the market. The philosophical presupposition of the prosopopoeia of the market involves more than attributing speech. More often than not it involves a specific form of speech in which a third person singular agent speaks in an enigmatic speech behind which lies a profound will or intentionality that is never apparent to all. Such ideas about personhood and speech lie deep in the cultural and religious history of the West. The idea that speech involves an assumption of a depth and intention is perhaps as old as the identification of speech with intention and reason. It is no doubt because of this depth that such ideas are able to move around so smoothly.

The market, like God, is taken to speak, but it does not speak clearly. The prosopopoeia of the market offers not direct veridiction but a subtle, implied and mysterious truth that requires deciphering. If it were to speak clearly then anyone could understand it. Speaking in signs that have to be deciphered requires representatives who will speak for it. This is not just a God, but a quite particular one. If this is a god then even if its will is perfect it is a God with quite human frailties at the level of execution. Such a notion is a perfect lure with which to secure the idea that despite all of the outer signs of weakness there remains a perfect interior. All failings are then only apparent, resting only in the flawed execution of a perfect and benevolent plan. This is the universe of what Žižek identifies as the Kafkaesque defence of God, in which God is taken to be at once perfect yet subject to human failings. Thus it can be argued that 'There is a God; He is good, and answers our requests – the origin of evil, and of our misfortune, is just that He does not hear very well and often misunderstands our prayers'.[44]

The market that speaks presents much the same situation with a minor but important twist. This God is not hard of hearing but is rather not very articulate. The market can hear us perfectly, it compiles our hopes and dreams and on this basis is in a position to guide our actions. But when it comes to advising us on what to do, this is a divinity that thunders in marvellous ways that somehow escape our limited understanding. This might be due to our incapacity to listen, but given the work on the side of decipherment it might well be said that this is a God who mumbles.

So if the market has over the past two or three centuries become a site of truth, this is a truth that remains forever enigmatic. It might seem that this is a rather strange form of speech to attribute to the market. But note that in this version of the prosopopoeia of the market perfection is still retained, not at the level of speech but at the level of intentionality. The market is thereby given something deeper and more profound than speech. Giving the market a pure will makes it possible to excuse it if, in its stumbling, clumsiness and mumbling, it might seem to our meagre and limited consciousness that it might get things wrong every now and then.

7

The invisible hand of Jupiter

If the market is a site of truth, a location in which truth is spoken, then it is not the market alone that speaks the truth. The market speaks a language that is complex, mysterious and oracular, so if the market is a site of veridiction then this site is dispersed and requires external agents who will be able to decipher its enigmatic yet profound speech. Truth resides somewhere between the speech of the market and the activity of those who might comprehend what the market is saying. The greater the puzzle and the more that the market remains a mystery, the greater the skill that can be imputed to those solving that puzzle, and with this, the greater the rewards for the fortunate few who can do the solving. Indeed, this forever mysterious nature of the market is one of the key answers as to the mystery of the prosopopoeia of the market. At the same time, this displacement of the location of truth is one of the truths about the market that the analysis of its prosopopoeia brings to light.

As Marieke de Goede has shown, the apparent irrationality of financial markets has played a vital function in conferring a corresponding rationality to those who trade on markets. This emerged in the historical construction of a binary relation between on the one hand the trader and on the other hand the market. It is through this relation between the trader and the market that the identity and character of the trader was able to be established and maintained. This is one of the reasons why shared fantasies about the market are so important. The irrationality of the market sustains the apparent rationality of those who might master its changeable and capricious nature. Casting the market as irrational also involves a complex set of assumptions about the gender of the market, as de Goede has also identified. The idea that the market might be a woman who is fickle yet powerful can therefore be mobilised to support claims to masculinity of those who might know and charm or even master her.[45]

Given what has been said about the specific form of the prosopopoeia of the market, it is possible to shed further light on the physical human characteristics that are attributed to the market. This will help to further clarify how the prosopopoeia of the market operates. Here again the motif of intentionality is crucial. When the market is taken to possess physical human capacities, these tend to be the organs that are most easily identifiable as intentional and purposive. It is therefore no coincidence that when the market takes on physical form it is so often attributed the most human of organs, the hand. The hand is generally taken to be the quintessentially human organ, by contrast with the paw or the hoof, which are incapable of such a wide variety of uses and such obvious displays of human intelligence. As Hegel says 'The hand is the element wherein one essentially recognizes the human'.[46]

The hand with opposable thumb is both the historical cause and the daily sign of human intelligence, and brings with it significant presuppositions about consciousness, intentionality and will. The hand is governed by an agent of a particular kind, who exercises agency through the activity of the hand. The hand makes manifest the designs of an intelligent consciousness. At the same time, however, the hand is nevertheless known for its unreliability. Of all the senses, the sense of touch is among the least reliable sources of sense perception and has long been disparaged by contrast to the power and external verifiability of sight. Moreover, the hand guided by even the most careful consciousness can fail to deliver on its intentions. This is why the hand can be excused its consequences if it has been guided by a good will. Even if it causes great pain it may well be that the clumsy hand can be excused this doing. These are important grounds as to why hand and will presuppose one another, and how the complex connection between hand and will can excuse the market, against all the evidence that might lead one to think that the market had intentions that were far from benign.

The hand is a figure that can unite the celestial and the worldly. It is thought that the divine can act not only through words but also through the physical force of touch. Jesus cures through touch and has a material agency in which it is hoped that just to touch him might effect a cure. In Michelangelo's painting of *The Creation of Adam* in the Sistine Chapel the finger of God reaches out to create the first human being. In much the same way, the market plays in such interstitial spaces. The market is something outside of this world but also something that appears in its manifestations, which take the form of the actions of a hand that intervenes right here and now.

It is easy to dismiss the idea that the market has hands. This is often done along the lines of the direct dismissal of prosopopoeia and the pathetic fallacy that were discussed earlier. Joseph Stiglitz, for example, argues that 'one of the reasons that the invisible hand may be invisible is that it is simply not there'.[47] As with the easy dismissal of prosopopoeia and personification, such an argument, although clearly having some polemical force, is severely limited. There is in this hand a very manifest reality – it is possible to feel the hand of the market in a very real way. Equally, just because something is invisible does not mean that it does not have real material effects. With the analysis of any ideology it is not enough to say that its objects do not exist. What is important is to bring to light what rests behind this ideology. Again, rather than casting aside the forms of appearance of the market, the task is to understand what truths can be brought to light by more fully understanding ideas that are in so many other ways patently false.

The idea that the market has hands has roots in the ancient analogy between society and the body. Such images are found in

Plato and Hobbes and in many others. But crucially, the idea that the market might possess an 'invisible hand' is generally associated with the writings of Adam Smith. The invisible hand appears three times across Smith's work, although it is generally received from a passage in the *Wealth of Nations*. Here as elsewhere Smith's Christianity appears directly in the way he evokes the idea of a benevolent force that assures that all is as it should be on earth despite what us humans intend. He speaks of how a capitalist who, supporting domestic rather than foreign industry can do good at home although he is only seeking his own profit: 'he intends only his own security; by directing that industry in such a manner as its produce may be of the greatest value, he intends only his own gain, and he is in this, as in many other cases, led by an invisible hand to promote an end which was no part of his intention'.[48]

Here again intentions come to the fore, appearing no less than three times in this short and often quoted passage. As should be clear from what has been argued so far, this displacement of intentionality away from the capitalist is only possible in the context of the imagination that there is an external agency that takes care of the matter of intentions. At this moment this agency must not be God, who according to most teachings would brutally punish base human selfishness. The market, however, is freed from such religious encumbrances, and as the market takes on a character such that it can resolve the troublesome matter of human intentions, the capitalist is freed by the market of certain otherwise troubling questions regarding the morality of the motivation of particular forms of action.

When the invisible hand appears elsewhere in Smith's writing, a strangely similar magic is at play. Perhaps the most interesting and certainly the most significant of the occasions on which the invisible hand appears in Smith's work is in his *History of Astronomy*.[49] In this book, which is part of his never completed work on the principles of philosophy, Smith sought to understand the historical origins of the sentiments of wonder, surprise and admiration. His account of the emergence of philosophy out of superstition tells the story of the various challenges that the superstitious mind falls prey to as it invents mystical explanations for the irregular and unusual events of nature. Faced with an unruly and threatening world filled with apparent irregularities, peoples without a scientific mindset create all manner of fantasies and illusions to explain the world.

Smith describes how 'a savage' imagines the irregularities of nature to be governed by the operation of 'some intelligent, though invisible causes, of whose vengeance and displeasure they are either the signs or the effects'. He locates the origins of polytheism in the belief that a variety of gods are responsible for these irregularities, which are then attributed to 'that vulgar superstition which ascribes all the irregular events of nature to the favour or displeasure of intelligent, though invisible beings, to gods, daemons, witches, genii, fairies'.

It is in the context of this superstitious attribution of powers to 'some invisible and designing power' that the idea of the invisible hand appears. The hand here is the 'invisible hand of Jupiter', the god of the gods. This hand of Jupiter appears in such a way that 'thunder and lightening, storms and sunshine, those more irregular events, were ascribed to his favour, or his anger'. Smith is unequivocal in his attack on this form of explanation of events. He denounces such belief in the invisible hand as belonging to the 'lowest and most pusillanimous superstitions'.[50]

Superstitions such as this are pusillanimous in the precise sense that they are lacking in courage. For Smith, they lack the courage to face up to the tasks of observing, understanding and reasoning about the operation of seeming irregularities. They lack courage insofar as they project onto an external third party intentional force when in fact agency lies elsewhere. The irony is that it is so often in precisely such terms that actors in markets have attempted to absolve themselves of responsibility for the consequences of their actions, on the basis that a third party was supervening above their action with an invisible hand. In this abstraction of the market from relations between people, the market can become a thing, a unified 'it' whose intentions are ultimately for the good. This motif runs across various personifications and attempts to represent the market in an embodied physical form. Whether as Jupiter the god of gods or as 'the markets' that demand global austerity, individual intentions disappear and are externalised onto a supposedly benevolent will. In this lies the secret to what becomes invisible when it is imagined that the market is a unified body invested with a pure will and something like an invisible hand. What becomes invisible are those who suffer the consequences of this hand.

8

The violence of metonymy

The figure of the market is central in choices that today govern the distribution of resources, power and privilege and the ways in which particular human beings command the life chances of others. That this situation is political should be blindingly obvious. But the fact that the market is political does not explain the politics that accompany the figure of the market. Having established a sketch of the mode of existence of the complex cultural forms that come with the prosopopoeia and personification of the market, what now remains is to complete this account of what these symbolic forms do and to then move to the question of what might be done about them. These are questions about the specific politics that come with the prosopopoeia and personification of the market. If these politics have been put in the background until now, at the same time that the falsity of the idea that the market can speak has been set aside, this was in order to avoid leaping too quickly to judgement and instead setting the task of understanding as the vital first step.

That being said, politics was implicit in the psychoanalytic critique of the prosopopoeia of the market, which exposed the motivations that can rest behind attributing socially unspeakable motivations to an external agent. A second moment of this politics emerged from the critique of primary personification and the theological critique of the prosopopoeia of the market, which together clarified the way that the enigmatic speech of the market presupposes a select cadre of experts to decipher it, in a process which brings with it the systematic exclusion of specific others who would speak of the market and what it does. A third element of this politics emerged from the theme that has been clarified in the previous two chapters but has been implicit throughout, that is, the way that the alibi of the good intentions of the market is used to deter analysis of the motivations of market actors and the concrete consequences of markets. Here it is possible to go one step further and locate the particular politics associated with finding in the market a unified figure that speaks as One. Building on and working alongside the three previous critiques, this chapter introduces what can be called the *critique of the political violence of the prosopopoeia of the market*.

Central to the political violence of the prosopopoeia of the market is the linguistic figure of metonymy. Metonymy is the figure of language in which one aspect of a thing is given the name of the thing as a whole. Thus the expression 'the crown' is used to represent the powers of the Queen even though the crown is only one aspect of the queenly apparatus. Metonymy also occurs when, for example, particular brands of products are used to reflect all varieties of that product. Thus Hoover and Xerox are nouns referring to particular products that have later been taken up as verbs referring to vacuuming and photocopying in general.

In metonymy a part stands in for the whole. This is the linguistic equivalent by which a part can extend itself or, as some might say, claim hegemony over a social space. Metaphor finds similarities between particular and particular, saying that one thing or person is like another. By contrast, metonymy effects a short-circuit between the particular and the universal. Metonymy gives name and law (*nomos*) to others outside of the element of the particular. This is why metonymy is so central to politics.

Metonymy can be used to understand a number of forms of political speech. In many times and places, 'man' has been taken as a metonym of humanity, in a process whereby one part of humanity was taken to stand as the norm or standard for the whole. To contest this metonymic reduction is to contest the way that this particular (man) could presume to stand in the place of the universal (humanity). Similarly, one can see how often today 'the consumer' operates as a metonym of the desiring subject, seeking as it does to take a part of the life of desire and turn that part most amenable to capitalist expansion into the basis of social life.

To put the particular in the place of the universal always involves a certain violence, the violence of metonymy.[51] When a whole is so composed, there is a systematic logic of division, prioritisation and exclusion. This is a violence done to those elements that are not counted within the whole as full participants. In this miscounting or discounting of participants, there are market participants that are necessary to the market situation, for example through producing the goods and services which are sold on the market, but who, through the violence of metonymy, are included in the situation but not considered to belong to it.[52]

The market has a remarkable ability to expand metonymically, so as to stand in the place of the entire public sphere. This thing called the market is itself composed of a multiplicity of actors and for there to be a market there must be at least three actors, in that there must be more than one of either buyers or sellers.[53] But beyond this rather obvious fact is the issue that has emerged from consideration of the prosopopoeia and personification of the market, which is the symbolic figuration by which the abstract figure of the market stands in the place of an imagined whole.

This is why for there to be a market there must also be a 'name of the father', that is, an ordering, regulating symbolic authority that acts as a third party to any particular actors on the market. This is how actors on markets are able to meet in a manner that seems anonymous, because their direct relations are mediated through this apparently external agent that can be known as 'the market'. Market actors only appear to be not relating to one another and to be not communicating to one another because they relate to each other via this shared object of imagination.

The democratic appeal of the idea of the market lies in the ostensible freedom that everyone has to participate in the market. But the other side to this freedom is the fact that any conceivable market is characterised by distinction in the capacity to participate. In a market desires and demands must reflect not merely willingness or intention but an actual ability to participate in the market – that is, an ability to pay. Although in principle all can equally enter a market, all never actually equally *are* the market. And herein lies the particular violence of the representation of the market as a unified One. To do such is to present the figure of a unity, a speaking in one voice, when in fact there are many.

In this metonymy that finds a One in the place of the multiple, there is a definite reality to who belongs and who is included but does not belong. To find a will of the market that speaks in the voice of a singular command that others must follow is the express denial of the multiple, and the installation of the power of those who stand in the position of the One. Today individuals and nations are told that they must suffer in order to atone the markets. This is a particular form of the generalisation of the interests of those that gain most from such a metonymic extension.

The expression 'the market' is a euphemism, a polite way of saying things. But 'the market' translates as the interests of specific participants within the circuit of the accumulation of capital. Today industrial capitalists are euphemistically known as 'entrepreneurs' and finance capitalists are known as 'investors'. Industrial and finance capitalists expand their wealth on condition of the labour of others, while this expansion is presented as if money expands by its own motive power. The effort of invention and investment that is undertaken by the entrepreneur and the investor is presented in metonymic relation with the effort of those systematically not recognised for their invention and investment in the process of labour. This violence, which is the violence of misrecognition of the labour of others and is the basis of the violence of capitalism, is hidden in these euphemisms and in these metonymic reductions.

The personification of the market as a unified and singular person is more than just personification. It is not only that the market is being thought of as a person, but there is here a specific idea of what it means to be a person. This notion of personhood involved in the personification of the market – the idea of a singular, unified and intentional person – is directly at odds with the reality, which is that the market is the action of a multiple.

Scholarly debates around personhood through the twentieth century in psychoanalysis, phenomenology, structuralism, poststructuralism and feminism have made clear the arbitrary nature of the assumption that the normal human person is a distinct and unified One. This figure of the unified person is arbitrary in the sense that it is a convention, a manner of speaking. When it comes to the prosopopoeia and personification of the market this is not just arbitrary. This figure of the unified One that is the market is the scene of the occlusion of antagonism between parties to market transactions.

This violence of metonymy accompanies what can be called the fetishism of the market. Fetishism takes a range of quite different forms and degrees, even if a certain fetishism is a quite normal part of human psychic and social life. At the most simple a fetish operates in much the same way as metonymy, by fixating on a part and taking that part as the whole. In full flight, the leather boot fetishist is *only* stimulated by leather boots, in real or imagined form. In such a fetish, one potential object of desire metonymically covers the whole scope of desire.

The concept of fetishism has held a particular pride of place in the critique of political economy since Marx took up this idea in his critique of commodity fetishism. In commodity fetishism, one part of the existence of a commodity is taken as its entire existence. This happens when the external appearance of a commodity, which is clearly one aspect of its reality, is taken to be all that there is to it. In doing so, the realities of the labour that has gone into its production are obscured. These conditions of the production of the commodity disappear or fade into the background and instead only the most obviously physical form of appearance of the commodity comes into view. This dynamic is not restricted to commodity production, but to a general tendency towards fetishism under capitalism, involving, as Marx puts it, 'the definite social relation between men themselves which assumes here, for them, the fantastic form of a relation between things'.

What is important to grasp is how Marx stresses that capitalism does not merely involve a dehumanisation in which relations between people are reduced to relations between things. Capitalism clearly does 'reify' certain social processes, making social relations appear as relations between things, but it also involves a much more complex and subtle series of substitutions between people and people, things and things, and between things and people. This series of substitutions works both ways and involves, as Marx stressed 'the personification of things and the reification of persons'.[54]

Perhaps most importantly, capitalism involves substitutions in which social relations between people can themselves take on the form of things or persons. Herein lies one of the crucial keys for understanding what it means when the market is imagined to be a subject that can speak. In the prosopopoeia of the market relations between people – which is at base what a market is – are abstracted from those relations and then given a life of their own. From those relations between people and in the light of their complexity, it is imagined that a subjective agent might somehow stand outside of those relations in order to command them. This is not an objectified nightmare in which the world has become fully enlightened and thus spiritless. Rather, this is a dream world of religious spiritualism filled with imagined intending agents. Surrounded with invented persons, we live in what Marx so aptly described as 'an enchanted, perverted, topsy-turvy world, in which Monsieur le Capital and Madame la Terre do their ghost-walking as social characters and at the same time directly as mere things'.[55]

Fetishism involves the universalization of a particular point, in a fashion that follows the logic of the violence of metonymy. Žižek draws attention to 'a certain "fetishism" which is independent of the opposition between "people" and "objects": it designates the state in which the effect of a "structure", of a network, is (mis)perceived as the distinct property of an individual entity'.[56] In the idea of the market as a person or a subject that has intentionality, will and voice, there is a transformation of the nature of the relationships between people. There is also a transformation in the relationship between people and this entity 'the market' that has been taken as a subject.

The market is definite relations between people that appear here in the form of a relation between on the one hand people and on the other hand a third party that is invested with human and indeed superhuman powers. This is the truth that is expressed in roundabout fashion by the prosopopoeia of the market. This truth appears in a remarkably wide range of different personifications of the market, whether self-conscious or not, and whether seeking to criticise or to defend the market. This truth expresses something important about what it is to live in relation to powers that have separated themselves so far from the majority of humanity. When power is exercised from what is experienced as a stratospheric distance, it is not merely false to imagine that this power is an external force. When power seems united in its direction and when one is fully included in executing its wishes, it is not merely false to see it as a unified One.

At this level the prosopopoeia of the market reflects something that is far from false. The prosopopoeia of the market expresses what is inexpressible in polite company and in the euphemistic languages that dominate so many discussions of market realities today. In this elliptical and roundabout fashion, the prosopopoeia of the market says something that is true but that is rarely said directly and openly. The prosopopoeia of the market expresses the systematic exclusions and the inclusions without belonging that characterise our age and which are experienced as the result of an uncontrollable economic process. In short, the prosopopoeia of the market speaks out loud the truth about the constantly expanding violence of contemporary capitalism.

9

The great disappearing trick

In late 2008 and into 2009 when financial markets were wreaking havoc across the globe, there were constant calls to placate the markets, and again today the markets are demanding austerity and fiscal restraint. When in late 2011 the elected governments of Italy and Greece were deposed by unelected financial technocrats, it was said that the markets had demanded such action. The markets then variously 'responded cautiously' or 'responded positively' to actions such as the installation of a technocratic government in Italy and the refusal to allow a referendum of the Greek people.[57]

Above all of this talking it was often hard to hear the many challenges that were being put to the market, which identified the pain that was being inflicted in its name at the same time that corporate profits and banking bonuses continued unabated. When such challenges started to rise, the market pulled what can be described as the great disappearing trick. When there was criticism of the market mechanism as such, and it was suggested that the market might be a cover up for systematic dispossession, the market itself vanished into thin air.

This disappearance presents serious problems for any critic that would challenge the actions of the market. The market plays out not simply in the register of the spoken and the silent but also in the visible and the invisible. When faced with the uncomfortable realities that seem to directly result from the actions of markets, either those realities or the fact that the market might be their cause are hidden from view.

The critical strategy of *the negative personification of the market* strikes against this disappearance. This strategy operates by casting the market in negative terms. This happens when, for example, the market is portrayed as a monster or as a person with monstrous, cruel or vindictive characteristics, such as when Marx speaks of capital as being vampire-like, or when he personifies capital in the figure of 'Our friend Moneybags'.[58] This kind of negative personification of the market is central to Joel Bakan's critical analysis of the attribution of personhood to the corporation. Bakan notes the legal attribution of personhood to corporations, and asks: if the corporation is a person, then what kind of person is it? His conclusion is that the corporation is a psychopath. This is not to argue that corporations are run by psychopaths or that corporations encourage psychopathic behaviours. Rather, Bakan argues that the corporation itself is psychopathological. Comparing the characteristics of corporations with those of clinical criteria of psychopathology, he notes that corporations are self-interested, unable to feel concern for others, are irresponsible, manipulative, grandiose, lack empathy, display asocial tendencies, refuse to accept responsibility and remorse, and relate to others superficially. These, he concludes, are also the characteristics of psychopaths.[59]

This strategy of negative personification of the market tends to rest on one form or another of the arguments from theology regarding theodicy or the 'problem of evil'. Such arguments generally note that the claims that God is both omnipotent and benevolent are contradicted by the realities of suffering. The critique will often commence by pointing to the state of the world that was claimed to be created by God and show how this is contradicted by claims as to God's nature.

Consider for example the Christian hymn *All Things Bright and Beautiful*, of which the first verse runs:

All things bright and beautiful
All creatures great and small
All things wise and wonderful
The Lord God made them all.[60]

The rather obvious response to the optimism of this song appears by completing the elements left out of this picture and attributing these to God. Thus Monty Python's parody of this hymn, in their song *All Things Dull and Ugly*:

> All things sick and cancerous
> All evil great and small
> All things foul and dangerous
> The Lord God made them all.[61]

The problem with this parody is that it faces a well practiced response, and this response can be taken up whether the problem of evil is put to belief in God or the market. This response is to assert that although the world does include the sick and cancerous as well as the bright and the beautiful, this is all for the best, either now, or in the long, long run. The most perfect of intentions are said to escape our limited understandings. It is said that although the market inflicts brutal costs on the people – whether in structural adjustment and austerity measures or in what is suffered while waiting for the market to finally deliver its bounty – this is ultimately and on the balance the best of all possible options.

Alternatively, the proponent of evil can respond by arguing that there is a higher purpose to suffering. In religious terms, it can be argued that suffering in this world is compensated in the next, or that freedom of the human will is such a great good that it justifies a certain level of suffering. In economic terms, it is argued that there is a higher good to which economic suffering must be compared. Inequality, for example, might not be desirable, but it serves a higher purpose, serving to motivate and to reward effort. To question the inequality produced by the market is to question such higher and nobler goals.

These are the very real arguments that are daily used to justify avoidable suffering. They all involve shifting focus, so that what was previously given credit for good deeds all of a sudden, when subjected to criticism, disappears. As has been intimated, this disappearance of the market involves a more profound disappearance, in the form of the disqualification from speech of those who might suffer at the hands of the market. Across the variety of versions of the disappearance of the market when called to account, the voices of those calling the market to account disappear or are not recognised as meaningful speech.

One of the ways that the great disappearing trick can operate, which has been seen many times in recent years, is to shift criticism of the market away from the market and onto the actions of particular individuals within the market. If it is possible to locate one or several participants in the market to take the fall then the market can be absolved of responsibility. Here the disappearing trick works by substitution or displacement. Following the financial crisis of 2008 this strategy has worked by identifying greedy bankers or 'fat cats'. In the removal of these particular individuals, the market is cleansed of those who diverted from the apparently normal functioning of the market. The fact that so much attention is paid to psychological motivations such as greed is indicative of this individualisation and the way that this serves to protect the market in the face of the reality of its operation.

Another way in which the great disappearing trick works is in the literal disappearance of the market as explanation or cause. The market has often figured in the popular imaginary as a strange sort of mysterious absence, as something both powerful yet ephemeral, present yet absent, having hands which must remain invisible. There is a long history of the notion that the market or aspects of the market have an ontologically negative character. Thus in 1709, Daniel Defoe wrote:

That substantial Non-entity call'd CREDIT, seems to have a distinct essence (if nothing can be said to exist) from all the

Phænomena in Nature; it is in it self the lightest and most volatile Body in the World, moveable beyond the Swiftness of Lightning; the greatest Alchymists could never fix its mercury, or find out its Quality; it is neither a Soul or a Body; it is neither visible or invisible; it is all Consequence, and yet not the Effect of a Cause; it is a Being without Matter, a Substance without Form.[62]

Defoe was writing at the moment of the rise of the market and the financial markets in particular. He and his work are important for the insight they offer into the nature of the mysterious character of the market, and the simultaneous appearance in concrete form, as noted earlier, of figures such as Lady Credit. That Defoe is important in the creation of the modern form of the fiction novel, in which self-conscious fictionalisation and the play of imaginary inventions take centre stage, is no coincidence. In her book on Defoe, Sandra Sherman has stressed the coincidence between the fictional form and the character of capitalism, the indeterminacy, perpetual uncertainty and instability of the market.[63]

The market exists in this switching between appearance and disappearance. As such, the market has neither presence nor absence. It is in the mobility of the ontological forms of the market that it is possible to register the ontology of the market, in this switching between the most abstract and the most concrete. The form of appearance of the market equally involves its disappearance, which is effected strategically when under threat. This is why I have argued elsewhere that the rise of the market gives birth to a particular experience of injury that knows no author. In such phenomena there is oppression without identifiable oppressor, mastery without master, a despotism without despot.[64]

10

Barbarians

The question 'Can the market speak?' clearly evokes the title of an important paper by Gayatri Chakravorty Spivak with the title 'Can the Subaltern Speak?'. In her paper Spivak poses profound challenges regarding the difficult task of representing the downtrodden and dispossessed, and above all those who are subjected in multiple ways. The subaltern are those in the weakest or worst position of society, and above all, those with the least capacity to do anything about it. They are the least able to express in the language of the dominant the reality of their dispossession.[65]

Silencing can be done by others and it can be done to oneself. The other can refuse to recognise one's speech, or on the other hand, one can find it conceptually or grammatically impossible to construct sentences that can confront and transform one's situation. As Spivak explains 'once a woman performs an act of resistance without an infrastructure that would make us recognize resistance, her resistance is in vain'.[66] This is the true cost of dispossession. It is not simply to exist on the margins but to be reduced to being the bystander to one's life or to be told that one's function is to watch and to work but not to speak. One can then mutter a cynical aside under one's breath, but there is no language in which to express the sense that one, one's people or one's world have been wronged. As Lyotard says: 'It is in the nature of the victim not to be able to prove that one has been done a wrong'.[67]

In his *Politics*, Aristotle posits that 'man is by nature a political animal'. The reason for this, he argues, is that 'man is the only animal who has the gift of speech'.[68] What Aristotle and so many who have followed him fail to register adequately is the equally human practice of the coding of human speech as speech. This is crucial because this process is central to the contemporary politics of dispossession. To be treated as a speaking subject requires more than that one open one's mouth. It requires a cultural and political decision over which speech will be qualified as speech and which will be disqualified.

The ancient Greeks distinguished between those endowed with the gift of speech and those who make sounds that only appear to be speech. One who could not speak Greek, and thus whose language sounded not like words but grunts and groans, did not qualify as being a true bearer of speech. The language of foreigners sounded to Greek ears not like real speech but nothing more than the sounds 'bar, bar, bar...', and so these foreigners were designated as 'barbarians'. Although today the word barbarian is used to designate someone uncultured or uncivilised, it was originally used in this way to designate the non-Greek, and later the non-Roman and the pagan.

Before a body is able to demand equality of participation it must demand that its speech be recognised as more than grunting and groaning. It must insist on the right to be heard as a speaking subject. Based on this important idea, Jacques Rancière has clearly articulated the way that politics is not a conflict between two or more equal parties of speech, but is rather a matter of claiming participation – that one can speak in a context in which one did not previously count as a participant.[69]

In the second half of the twentieth century the social sciences witnessed what has been called a 'linguistic turn'. At a certain point in the life of the university, almost everything became speech and discourse. Clearly, language is one of the things that there is in the world, even if it is not the only thing. Against this academic fashion to find language everywhere, one of the scholarly points that I have sought to make with this book is that there are serious risks with focusing on what is presented as speech. When something appears to be speech, what is most vital is the conditions of the coding of this speech as speech and the politics of this operation. Beyond the appearance of what is said is the demand that one think the conditions of presentation of speech.

Another scholarly argument of this book has been to stress the way that presuppositions about personhood are invariably smuggled in with the idea of speaking. This appeared throughout in the complex connection between speech and the attribution of intentionality. In this sense I should be clear that this project continues and extends the critique of what Jacques Derrida called 'phonocentrism', that is, the privilege of voice (*phōnē*) and in particular the place in this of the presupposition of 'the absolute proximity of voice and being, of voice and the meaning of being, of voice and the ideality of meaning'.[70] Above all I have sought to clarify the way that the prosopopoeia of the market brings with it a sense of an intending agent, and with this quite particular ideas about how that agent might function. This specific form of the market, which is central although of course not universal, is the idea of the market as unified, singular and external, with intentions that are always mysterious and require deciphering, and who can disappear if ever challenged.

Capitalism today appears to involve an elevation of speech and consciousness. This has been registered in a range of work on communicative, linguistic and affective labour and in discussions of what is known as cognitive capitalism. To this recognition of speech and consciousness must be added that capitalism involves a twin process of firstly seeking to capture or harvest useful speech for its own purposes and secondly to reduce those not useful to it to the status of senseless mutterers. No matter how articulate they might sound to others, they make no sense within the calculative logic of the market and their demands for justice simply cannot be understood. While capitalism fundamentally involves language, it is in this and other significant respects *alinguistic*, in that its central operations take place before or outside of the circuits of meaningful communicative speech.[71]

The configuration of speaking bodies so that the speech of many is reduced to nothing is one of the more significant ways in which capitalism is sociopathological. Capitalism contains a logic whereby economic imperatives come to talk over and to speak for other possible ways of deliberating on collective purpose. In this process, voices that express or make alternative proposals are thereby reduced to grunting and groaning. This is central to the depoliticisation that comes with capitalism, the fact that it takes control of economic matters out of speech and human intercourse. At best it codes speech in the language of the market, and that language denigrates all other languages as degenerate and inferior if not outright incomprehensible.

The capacity of speech is central to the politics of our age, but this politics is not restricted to language. There is a coding of speech as non-speech and as non-sense and there is an attribution elsewhere of speech to fantastic entities such as the market. This is not to say that all voices are of equal veridical or moral value. Far from it. If progressive politics for some years rested on the presupposition of equivalence of all voices, there is today a sense of the urgency of shaking self-imposed silences and the raising of voices. The dispossessions of our age are, paradoxically, making it not only possible but necessary to say directly that it is our masters who are speaking nonsense and that it is they and not we who are the barbarians.

Emerging out of the collective dispossession of our human capacities to sense and to speak it is thus possible to see growing signs today that it is time to speak. We are led to imagine that it is not unreasonable to demand the right to speak, firstly because there is something in what we say that is systematically unaccounted for by what is called the market. We then step forward and suggest, cautiously at first, that the market is not a thing, a person or a God. We assert that living has a value that the market cannot measure, that we and our world are not for sale, and that we can indeed speak and debate about the value of things outside of the chatter of the market. With growing confidence at last we begin to say that the market, or rather, those hiding behind it, cannot hide any longer. We have heard the market speak, we have laughed and cried at what it has done. Finally, and before it is too late, it is our turn to have the courage to learn how to speak.

Notes

1. John Maynard Keynes, *The General Theory of Employment Interest and Money* (London: Macmillan, 1967), p. 161. See also, for example, George Akerlof and Robert Shiller, *Animal Spirits: How Human Psychology Drives the Economy, and Why it Matters for Capitalism* (Princeton, NJ: Princeton University Press, 2009).

2. Benedict de Spinoza, *Ethics*, trans. Edwin Curley (London: Penguin, 1996), p. 4.

3. Karl Marx, *Capital: A Critique of Political Economy, Volume One*, trans. Ben Fowkes (London: Penguin, 1976), p. 90.

4. G. W. F. Hegel, *Phenomenology of Spirit* (Oxford: Oxford University Press, 1977), p. 208.

5. Max Weber, *The Protestant Ethic and the Spirit of Capitalism* (Oxford: Routledge, 2001), p. 121; Luc Boltanski and Ève Chiapello, *The New Spirit of Capitalism* (London: Verso, 2005).

6. Randy Martin, 'The twin towers of financialization: Entanglements of political and cultural economies' *The Global South*, 3(1), 2009, pp. 108-125.

7. 'IMF: World economy enters dangerous new phase'. Online at www.youtube.com/watch?v=kGZjz2d8Qrk

8. 'Have PhD, will govern' *The Economist*, 16 November 2011. Online at www.economist.com/blogs/newsbook/2011/11/technocrats-and-democracy

9. Sydney Tremayne, *How to Become a Wealthy Investor: Listen to the Market and it Will Tell You What to Do* (Kindle Editions, 2011); Jelynne Jardiniano, *Restaurant from Scratch: How to Trust Your Heart, Listen to the Market and Beat the Odds* (Roswell, GA: Advantage Media, 2011).

10. Mark Manning, 'Listen to what the market is telling you'. Online at http://www.tradingmarkets.com/.site/stocks/how _to/articles/Listen-to-What-the-Market-is-Telling-You-

80222.cfm.

11. I document some of this personification of the market in 'What kind of subject is the market?', *New Formations*, (2011), 72: 131-144.

12. Robert Smitley, *Popular Financial Delusions*, Philadelphia, Roland Swain Company, 1933, p. 8.

13. Adam Smith (pseudonym for Georg Goodman), *The Money Game*, New York, Random House, 1967, p. 23.

14. Urs Stäheli, *Spektakuläre Spekulation: Das Populäre der Ökonomie* (Berlin, Suhrkamp, 2007) p. 289.

15. Marx, *op cit.*, pp. 375, 176.

16. Marx, *op cit.*, p. 92. See also pp. 254 and 265.

17. Michael Hardt and Antonio Negri, *Commonwealth* (Harvard, MA: Harvard University Press, 2009), p. 300.

18. American Psychiatric Association, *Diagnostic and Statistical Manual of Mental Disorders, Fourth Edition, Text Revision, DSMIV-TR* (Washington, DC: American Psychiatric Association, 2000) p. 823.

19. Keynes, *op cit.*, p. 383.

20. Jonathan Rée, *I See a Voice: Language, Deafness and the Senses – A Philosophical History* (London: HarperCollins, 1999), p. 44, 48, 47.

21. See Daniel B. Smith, *Muses, Madmen and Prophets: Hearing Voices and the Borders of Sanity* (New York: Penguin, 2007).

22. Daniel Paul Schreber, *Memoirs of My Nervous Illness*, trans. and ed. Ida MacAlpine and Richard Hunter (New York: New York Review Books, 2000).

23. Sigmund Freud, 'Psychoanalytic notes on an autobiographical account of a case of paranoia (dementia paranoides)' in *Standard Edition of the Complete Psychological Works of Sigmund Freud*, vol. XII, trans. James Strachey (London: Hogarth, 1958).

24. Sigmund Freud, *The Interpretation of Dreams* in *Standard Edition of the Complete Psychological Works of Sigmund Freud*,

vol. IV, trans. James Strachey (London: Hogarth, 1953), p. 122.

25. Jacques Lacan, *The Psychoses: The Seminar of Jacques Lacan, Book III, 1955-1956*, trans. Russell Grigg (London: Routledge, 1993), pp. 92, 96.

26. Michel Foucault, *The Order of Things* (London: Routledge, 1970).

27. Quintilian, *The Orator's Education, Books 9-10* (Cambridge, MA: Harvard University Press, 2001), p. 51.

28. Quintilian, *ibid*.

29. Samuel Taylor Coleridge, 'Christabel' in *The Complete Poems* (London: Penguin, 1997), p. 187.

30. John Ruskin, *Modern Painters, Volume Three* (London: Dent, 1905), p. 149.

31. Paul de Man, *The Rhetoric of Romanticism* (New York: Columbia University Press, 1984), p. 122.

32. Michel Foucault, 'What is an author?' in *Language, Counter-Memory, Practice*, ed. Donald Bouchard (Ithaca, NY: Cornell University Press, 1977), p. 138.

33. See, for example, Harvey Fox, 'The market as God: Living in the new dispensation' *Atlantic Monthly*, March 1999.

34. South Park 'Margaritaville', Season 13, Episode 3. First televised 25 March 2009.

35. Carl Schmitt, *Political Theology*, trans. George Schwab (Chicago: University of Chicago, 1985), p. 36.

36. Friedrich Nietzsche, *The Gay Science*, trans. Walter Kaufmann (New York: Vintage, 1974), p. 108.

37. Foucault, *The Order of Things*, p. 385.

38. Michel Foucault, *The Birth of Biopolitics: Lectures at the Collège de France, 1978-79*, trans. Graham Burchill (Basingstoke: Palgrave Macmillan, 2008), p. 32.

39. Walter Benjamin, 'On the concept of history' in *Selected Writings: Volume 4, 1938-1940*, trans. Edmund Jeffcott et al. (Harvard, MA: Harvard University Press, 2003), p. 389.

40. Mladen Dolar, *A Voice and Nothing More* (Harvard, MA: Harvard University Press, 2006), pp. 10, 7-8.
41. Theodor Adorno, *The Stars Down to Earth and Other Essays on the Irrational in Culture* (London: Routledge, 1994), p. 36.
42. Alex Preda, *Framing Finance: The Boundaries of Markets and Modern Capitalism* (Chicago, University of Chicago Press, 2009).
43. Christian Marazzi, *The Violence of Financial Capitalism* (New York: Semiotext(e), 2010), p. 99.
44. Slavoj Žižek, *The Puppet and the Dwarf: The Perverse Core of Christianity* (Harvard, MA: MIT Press, 2003), p. 89.
45. Marieke de Goede, *Virtue, Fortune and Faith: A Genealogy of Finance* (Minneapolis, MN: University of Minnesota Press, 2005).
46. Georg Wilhelm Friedrich Hegel, *Lectures on the Philosophy of Spirit, 1827-8*, trans. Robert Williams (Oxford: Oxford University Press, 2007), p. 160. See also Hegel, *Phenomenology*, p. 189.
47. Joseph Stiglitz, *The Roaring Nineties* (London: Penguin, 2004), p. 13.
48. Adam Smith, *The Wealth of Nations, Books IV-V*, ed. Andrew Skinner (London: Penguin, 1999), p. 32.
49. In addition to the uses cited above and below, see Adam Smith, *The Theory of Moral Sentiments* (Amerherst, NY: Prometheus, 2000), p. 264.
50. Adam Smith, 'The history of astronomy' in *Essays on Philosophical Subjects* (Oxford: Oxford University Press, 1980), p. 48, 49, 50.
51. This idea is drawn from Jacques Derrida, *Specters of Marx*, trans. Peggy Kamuf (New York: Routledge, 1994), p. xv.
52. On this logic see Alain Badiou, *Being and Event*, trans. Oliver Feltham (London: Continuum, 2005).
53. Patrik Aspers, *Markets* (Oxford: Polity, 2011), p. 7.
54. Karl Marx, *Capital: A Critique of Political Economy, Volume One*,

trans. Ben Fowkes (London, Penguin, 1976), pp. 165, 1054.

55. Karl Marx, *Capital: A Critique of Political Economy, Volume III*, (London: Lawrence and Wishart, 1972), p. 830.

56. Slavoj Žižek, *The Plague of Fantasies* (London: Verso, 1997), p. 100.

57. See for example, 'Italy crisis: Mario Monti moves to form new government', BBC News, 14 November 2011; 'Italy and Spain pass key bonds test' *The Telegraph*, 17 January 2012.

58. Karl Marx, *Capital: A Critique of Political Economy, Volume I*, trans. Samuel Moore and Edward Aveling (London: Lawrence and Wishart, 1954) pp. 163 and 169. Note that the figure of 'Our friend, moneybags' is translated out by Ben Fowkes in his translation. See Marx, *Capital: A Critique of Political Economy, Volume One*, trans. Ben Fowkes (London: Penguin, 1976), pp. 269 and 279.

59. Joel Bakan, *The Corporation: The Pathological Pursuit of Profit and Power* (London: Constable, 2004), pp. 56-57.

60. Cecil Frances Alexander, 'All things bright and beautiful', in *Hymns Ancient and Modern* (London: William Clowes and Sons, 1875), p. 447.

61. See *Monty Python's Contractual Obligation Album* (Charisma Records, 1980). An alternative critique of *All Things Bright and Beautiful* is to take the song in its entirety seriously. One could do this for instance by singing the third verse, which is generally omitted today. This verse reads 'The rich man in his castle/The poor man at his gate/God made them, high or lowly/And order'd their estate' (Alexander, *ibid.*).

62. Daniel Defoe, *A Review of the State of the British Nation*, 14 June 1709, vol. VI, no. 31.

63. Sandra Sherman, *Finance and Fictionality in the Early Eighteenth Century: Accounting for Defoe* (Cambridge: Cambridge University Press, 1996), pp. 72, 105, 112 and *passim*.

64. Campbell Jones, 'What kind of subject is the market?', *New*

Formations, (2011), 72: 131-144. Reprinted in David Bennett (ed) *Loaded Subjects; Psychoanalysis, Money and the Global Financial Crisis* (London: Lawrence & Wishart, 2012).

65. Gayatri Chakravorty Spivak, 'Can the subaltern speak?' in Cary Nelson and Lawrence Grossberg (eds.) *Marxism and the Interpretation of Culture* (Urbana, IL: University of Illinois Press, 1988). Revised and extended as chapter 3 of *A Critique of Postcolonial Reason* (Harvard, MA: Harvard University Press, 1999).

66. Gayatri Chakravorty Spivak, *Conversations with Gayatri Chakravorty Spivak* (London: Seagull, 2006), p. 62.

67. Jean-François Lyotard, *The Differend: Phrases in Dispute*, trans. Georges Van Den Abbeele (Minneapolis, MN: University of Minnesota Press, 1988), p. 8.

68. Aristotle, *Politics*, trans. B. Jowett, in Jonathan Barnes (ed.) *Complete Works* (Oxford: Oxford University Press, 1984), 1253a.

69. Jacques Rancière, 'Ten theses on politics' in *Dissensus*, trans. Steve Corcoran (London: Continuum, 2010).

70. Jacques Derrida, *Of Grammatology*, trans. Gayatri Chakravorty Spivak (Baltimore: Johns Hopkins University Press, 1976), p. 12.

71. On these dynamics see Boris Groys, *The Communist Postscript*, trans. Thomas Ford (London: Verso, 2009).

Contemporary culture has eliminated both the concept of the public and the figure of the intellectual. Former public spaces – both physical and cultural – are now either derelict or colonized by advertising. A cretinous anti-intellectualism presides, cheerled by expensively educated hacks in the pay of multinational corporations who reassure their bored readers that there is no need to rouse themselves from their interpassive stupor. The informal censorship internalized and propagated by the cultural workers of late capitalism generates a banal conformity that the propaganda chiefs of Stalinism could only ever have dreamt of imposing. Zer0 Books knows that another kind of discourse – intellectual without being academic, popular without being populist – is not only possible: it is already flourishing, in the regions beyond the striplit malls of so-called mass media and the neurotically bureaucratic halls of the academy. Zer0 is committed to the idea of publishing as a making public of the intellectual. It is convinced that in the unthinking, blandly consensual culture in which we live, critical and engaged theoretical reflection is more important than ever before.